THE BALLAD OF READING GAOL, RAVENNA, & OTHER POEMS

OSCAR WILDE

CONTENTS

THE BALLAD OF READING GAOL

RAVENNA

ROSA MYSTICA

THE BURDEN OF ITYS

THE SPHINX

FLOWERS OF GOLD

THE BALLAD OF READING GAOL

I

He did not wear his scarlet coat,
  For blood and wine are red,
And blood and wine were on his hands
  When they found him with the dead,
The poor dead woman whom he loved,
  And murdered in her bed.

He walked amongst the Trial Men
  In a suit of shabby grey;
A cricket cap was on his head,
  And his step seemed light and gay;
But I never saw a man who looked
  So wistfully at the day.

I never saw a man who looked
  With such a wistful eye
Upon that little tent of blue
  Which prisoners call the sky,
And at every drifting cloud that went
  With sails of silver by.

I walked, with other souls in pain,
  Within another ring,
And was wondering if the man had done
  A great or little thing,

When a voice behind me whispered low,
  'That fellow's got to swing.'

Dear Christ! the very prison walls
  Suddenly seemed to reel,
And the sky above my head became
  Like a casque of scorching steel;
And, though I was a soul in pain,
  My pain I could not feel.

I only knew what hunted thought
  Quickened his step, and why
He looked upon the garish day
  With such a wistful eye;
The man had killed the thing he loved,
  And so he had to die.

Yet each man kills the thing he loves,
  By each let this be heard,
Some do it with a bitter look,
  Some with a flattering word,
The coward does it with a kiss,
  The brave man with a sword!

Some kill their love when they are young,
  And some when they are old;
Some strangle with the hands of Lust,
  Some with the hands of Gold:
The kindest use a knife, because
  The dead so soon grow cold.

Some love too little, some too long,
  Some sell, and others buy;
Some do the deed with many tears,
  And some without a sigh:
For each man kills the thing he loves,
  Yet each man does not die.

He does not die a death of shame
  On a day of dark disgrace,

Nor have a noose about his neck,
    Nor a cloth upon his face,
Nor drop feet foremost through the floor
    Into an empty space.

❧

He does not sit with silent men
    Who watch him night and day;
Who watch him when he tries to weep,
    And when he tries to pray;
Who watch him lest himself should rob
    The prison of its prey.

He does not wake at dawn to see
    Dread figures throng his room,
The shivering Chaplain robed in white,
    The Sheriff stern with gloom,
And the Governor all in shiny black,
    With the yellow face of Doom.

He does not rise in piteous haste
    To put on convict-clothes,
While some coarse-mouthed Doctor gloats, and notes
    Each new and nerve-twitched pose,
Fingering a watch whose little ticks
    Are like horrible hammer-blows.

He does not know that sickening thirst
    That sands one's throat, before
The hangman with his gardener's gloves
    Slips through the padded door,
And binds one with three leathern thongs,
    That the throat may thirst no more.

He does not bend his head to hear
    The Burial Office read,
Nor, while the terror of his soul
    Tells him he is not dead,
Cross his own coffin, as he moves
    Into the hideous shed.

He does not stare upon the air
  Through a little roof of glass:
He does not pray with lips of clay
  For his agony to pass;
Nor feel upon his shuddering cheek
  The kiss of Caiaphas.

II

Six weeks our guardsman walked the yard,
    In the suit of shabby grey:
His cricket cap was on his head,
    And his step seemed light and gay,
But I never saw a man who looked
    So wistfully at the day.

I never saw a man who looked
    With such a wistful eye
Upon that little tent of blue
    Which prisoners call the sky,
And at every wandering cloud that trailed
    Its ravelled fleeces by.

He did not wring his hands, as do
    Those witless men who dare
To try to rear the changeling Hope
    In the cave of black Despair:
He only looked upon the sun,
    And drank the morning air.

He did not wring his hands nor weep,
    Nor did he peek or pine,
But he drank the air as though it held
    Some healthful anodyne;
With open mouth he drank the sun

As though it had been wine!

And I and all the souls in pain,
  Who tramped the other ring,
Forgot if we ourselves had done
  A great or little thing,
And watched with gaze of dull amaze
  The man who had to swing.

And strange it was to see him pass
  With a step so light and gay,
And strange it was to see him look
  So wistfully at the day,
And strange it was to think that he
  Had such a debt to pay.

For oak and elm have pleasant leaves
  That in the springtime shoot:
But grim to see is the gallows-tree,
  With its adder-bitten root,
And, green or dry, a man must die
  Before it bears its fruit!

The loftiest place is that seat of grace
  For which all worldlings try:
But who would stand in hempen band
  Upon a scaffold high,
And through a murderer's collar take
  His last look at the sky?

It is sweet to dance to violins
  When Love and Life are fair:
To dance to flutes, to dance to lutes
  Is delicate and rare:
But it is not sweet with nimble feet
  To dance upon the air!

So with curious eyes and sick surmise
  We watched him day by day,
And wondered if each one of us
  Would end the self-same way,

For none can tell to what red Hell
  His sightless soul may stray.

At last the dead man walked no more
  Amongst the Trial Men,
And I knew that he was standing up
  In the black dock's dreadful pen,
And that never would I see his face
  In God's sweet world again.

Like two doomed ships that pass in storm
  We had crossed each other's way:
But we made no sign, we said no word,
  We had no word to say;
For we did not meet in the holy night,
  But in the shameful day.

A prison wall was round us both,
  Two outcast men we were:
The world had thrust us from its heart,
  And God from out His care:
And the iron gin that waits for Sin
  Had caught us in its snare.

In Debtors' Yard the stones are hard,
  And the dripping wall is high,
So it was there he took the air
  Beneath the leaden sky,
And by each side a Warder walked,
  For fear the man might die.

Or else he sat with those who watched
  His anguish night and day;
Who watched him when he rose to weep,
  And when he crouched to pray;
Who watched him lest himself should rob
  Their scaffold of its prey.

The Governor was strong upon
  The Regulations Act:
The Doctor said that Death was but
  A scientific fact:
And twice a day the Chaplain called,
  And left a little tract.

And twice a day he smoked his pipe,
  And drank his quart of beer:
His soul was resolute, and held
  No hiding-place for fear;
He often said that he was glad

The hangman's hands were near.

But why he said so strange a thing
  No Warder dared to ask:
For he to whom a watcher's doom
  Is given as his task,
Must set a lock upon his lips,
  And make his face a mask.

Or else he might be moved, and try
  To comfort or console:
And what should Human Pity do
  Pent up in Murderers' Hole?
What word of grace in such a place
  Could help a brother's soul?

With slouch and swing around the ring
  We trod the Fools' Parade!
We did not care: we knew we were
  The Devil's Own Brigade:
And shaven head and feet of lead
  Make a merry masquerade.

We tore the tarry rope to shreds
  With blunt and bleeding nails;
We rubbed the doors, and scrubbed the floors,
  And cleaned the shining rails:
And, rank by rank, we soaped the plank,
  And clattered with the pails.

We sewed the sacks, we broke the stones,
  We turned the dusty drill:
We banged the tins, and bawled the hymns,
  And sweated on the mill:
But in the heart of every man
  Terror was lying still.

So still it lay that every day
  Crawled like a weed-clogged wave:
And we forgot the bitter lot
  That waits for fool and knave,

Till once, as we tramped in from work,
　We passed an open grave.

With yawning mouth the yellow hole
　Gaped for a living thing;
The very mud cried out for blood
　To the thirsty asphalte ring:
And we knew that ere one dawn grew fair
　Some prisoner had to swing.

Right in we went, with soul intent
　On Death and Dread and Doom:
The hangman, with his little bag,
　Went shuffling through the gloom:
And each man trembled as he crept
　Into his numbered tomb.

That night the empty corridors
　Were full of forms of Fear,
And up and down the iron town
　Stole feet we could not hear,
And through the bars that hide the stars
　White faces seemed to peer.

He lay as one who lies and dreams
　In a pleasant meadow-land,
The watchers watched him as he slept,
　And could not understand
How one could sleep so sweet a sleep
　With a hangman close at hand.

But there is no sleep when men must weep
　Who never yet have wept:
So we—the fool, the fraud, the knave—
　That endless vigil kept,
And through each brain on hands of pain
　Another's terror crept.

Alas! it is a fearful thing
　To feel another's guilt!
For, right within, the sword of Sin

Pierced to its poisoned hilt,
And as molten lead were the tears we shed
 For the blood we had not spilt.

The Warders with their shoes of felt
 Crept by each padlocked door,
And peeped and saw, with eyes of awe,
 Grey figures on the floor,
And wondered why men knelt to pray
 Who never prayed before.

All through the night we knelt and prayed,
 Mad mourners of a corse!
The troubled plumes of midnight were
 The plumes upon a hearse:
And bitter wine upon a sponge
 Was the savour of Remorse.

The grey cock crew, the red cock crew,
 But never came the day:
And crooked shapes of Terror crouched,
 In the corners where we lay:
And each evil sprite that walks by night
 Before us seemed to play.

They glided past, they glided fast,
 Like travellers through a mist:
They mocked the moon in a rigadoon
 Of delicate turn and twist,
And with formal pace and loathsome grace
 The phantoms kept their tryst.

With mop and mow, we saw them go,
 Slim shadows hand in hand:
About, about, in ghostly rout
 They trod a saraband:
And the damned grotesques made arabesques,
 Like the wind upon the sand!

With the pirouettes of marionettes,
 They tripped on pointed tread:
But with flutes of Fear they filled the ear,
 As their grisly masque they led,

And loud they sang, and long they sang,
   For they sang to wake the dead.

'Oho!' they cried, 'The world is wide,
   But fettered limbs go lame!
And once, or twice, to throw the dice
   Is a gentlemanly game,
But he does not win who plays with Sin
   In the secret House of Shame.'

No things of air these antics were,
   That frolicked with such glee:
To men whose lives were held in gyves,
   And whose feet might not go free,
Ah! wounds of Christ! they were living things,
   Most terrible to see.

Around, around, they waltzed and wound;
   Some wheeled in smirking pairs;
With the mincing step of a demirep
   Some sidled up the stairs:
And with subtle sneer, and fawning leer,
   Each helped us at our prayers.

The morning wind began to moan,
   But still the night went on:
Through its giant loom the web of gloom
   Crept till each thread was spun:
And, as we prayed, we grew afraid
   Of the Justice of the Sun.

The moaning wind went wandering round
   The weeping prison-wall:
Till like a wheel of turning steel
   We felt the minutes crawl:
O moaning wind! what had we done
   To have such a seneschal?

At last I saw the shadowed bars,
   Like a lattice wrought in lead,
Move right across the whitewashed wall
   That faced my three-plank bed,
And I knew that somewhere in the world

God's dreadful dawn was red.

At six o'clock we cleaned our cells,
  At seven all was still,
But the sough and swing of a mighty wing
  The prison seemed to fill,
For the Lord of Death with icy breath
  Had entered in to kill.

He did not pass in purple pomp,
  Nor ride a moon-white steed.
Three yards of cord and a sliding board
  Are all the gallows' need:
So with rope of shame the Herald came
  To do the secret deed.

We were as men who through a fen
  Of filthy darkness grope:
We did not dare to breathe a prayer,
  Or to give our anguish scope:
Something was dead in each of us,
  And what was dead was Hope.

For Man's grim Justice goes its way,
  And will not swerve aside:
It slays the weak, it slays the strong,
  It has a deadly stride:
With iron heel it slays the strong,
  The monstrous parricide!

We waited for the stroke of eight:
  Each tongue was thick with thirst:
For the stroke of eight is the stroke of Fate
  That makes a man accursed,
And Fate will use a running noose
  For the best man and the worst.

We had no other thing to do,
  Save to wait for the sign to come:
So, like things of stone in a valley lone,
  Quiet we sat and dumb:
But each man's heart beat thick and quick,
  Like a madman on a drum!

With sudden shock the prison-clock
  Smote on the shivering air,
And from all the gaol rose up a wail
  Of impotent despair,
Like the sound that frightened marshes hear
  From some leper in his lair.

And as one sees most fearful things
  In the crystal of a dream,
We saw the greasy hempen rope
  Hooked to the blackened beam,
And heard the prayer the hangman's snare
  Strangled into a scream.

And all the woe that moved him so
  That he gave that bitter cry,
And the wild regrets, and the bloody sweats,
  None knew so well as I:
For he who lives more lives than one
  More deaths than one must die.

IV

There is no chapel on the day
  On which they hang a man:
The Chaplain's heart is far too sick,
  Or his face is far too wan,
Or there is that written in his eyes
  Which none should look upon.

So they kept us close till nigh on noon,
  And then they rang the bell,
And the Warders with their jingling keys
  Opened each listening cell,
And down the iron stair we tramped,
  Each from his separate Hell.

Out into God's sweet air we went,
  But not in wonted way,
For this man's face was white with fear,
  And that man's face was grey,
And I never saw sad men who looked
  So wistfully at the day.

I never saw sad men who looked
  With such a wistful eye
Upon that little tent of blue
  We prisoners called the sky,
And at every careless cloud that passed

In happy freedom by.

But there were those amongst us all
  Who walked with downcast head,
And knew that, had each got his due,
  They should have died instead:
He had but killed a thing that lived,
  Whilst they had killed the dead.

For he who sins a second time
  Wakes a dead soul to pain,
And draws it from its spotted shroud,
  And makes it bleed again,
And makes it bleed great gouts of blood,
  And makes it bleed in vain!

Like ape or clown, in monstrous garb
  With crooked arrows starred,
Silently we went round and round
  The slippery asphalte yard;
Silently we went round and round,
  And no man spoke a word.

Silently we went round and round,
  And through each hollow mind
The Memory of dreadful things
  Rushed like a dreadful wind,
And Horror stalked before each man,
  And Terror crept behind.

The Warders strutted up and down,
  And kept their herd of brutes,
Their uniforms were spick and span,
  And they wore their Sunday suits,
But we knew the work they had been at,
  By the quicklime on their boots.

For where a grave had opened wide,
  There was no grave at all:

Only a stretch of mud and sand
　By the hideous prison-wall,
And a little heap of burning lime,
　That the man should have his pall.

For he has a pall, this wretched man,
　Such as few men can claim:
Deep down below a prison-yard,
　Naked for greater shame,
He lies, with fetters on each foot,
　Wrapt in a sheet of flame!

And all the while the burning lime
　Eats flesh and bone away,
It eats the brittle bone by night,
　And the soft flesh by day,
It eats the flesh and bone by turns,
　But it eats the heart alway.

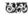

For three long years they will not sow
　Or root or seedling there:
For three long years the unblessed spot
　Will sterile be and bare,
And look upon the wondering sky
　With unreproachful stare.

They think a murderer's heart would taint
　Each simple seed they sow.
It is not true! God's kindly earth
　Is kindlier than men know,
And the red rose would but blow more red,
　The white rose whiter blow.

Out of his mouth a red, red rose!
　Out of his heart a white!
For who can say by what strange way,
　Christ brings His will to light,
Since the barren staff the pilgrim bore
　Bloomed in the great Pope's sight?

But neither milk-white rose nor red

May bloom in prison-air;
The shard, the pebble, and the flint,
   Are what they give us there:
For flowers have been known to heal
   A common man's despair.

So never will wine-red rose or white,
   Petal by petal, fall
On that stretch of mud and sand that lies
   By the hideous prison-wall,
To tell the men who tramp the yard
   That God's Son died for all.

Yet though the hideous prison-wall
   Still hems him round and round,
And a spirit may not walk by night
   That is with fetters bound,
And a spirit may but weep that lies
   In such unholy ground,

He is at peace—this wretched man—
   At peace, or will be soon:
There is no thing to make him mad,
   Nor does Terror walk at noon,
For the lampless Earth in which he lies
   Has neither Sun nor Moon.

They hanged him as a beast is hanged:
   They did not even toll
A requiem that might have brought
   Rest to his startled soul,
But hurriedly they took him out,
   And hid him in a hole.

They stripped him of his canvas clothes,
   And gave him to the flies:
They mocked the swollen purple throat,
   And the stark and staring eyes:
And with laughter loud they heaped the shroud
   In which their convict lies.

The Chaplain would not kneel to pray
  By his dishonoured grave:
Nor mark it with that blessed Cross
  That Christ for sinners gave,
Because the man was one of those
  Whom Christ came down to save.

Yet all is well; he has but passed
  To Life's appointed bourne:
And alien tears will fill for him
  Pity's long-broken urn,
For his mourners will be outcast men,
  And outcasts always mourn

V

I know not whether Laws be right,
  Or whether Laws be wrong;
All that we know who lie in gaol
  Is that the wall is strong;
And that each day is like a year,
  A year whose days are long.

But this I know, that every Law
  That men have made for Man,
Since first Man took his brother's life,
  And the sad world began,
But straws the wheat and saves the chaff
  With a most evil fan.

This too I know—and wise it were
  If each could know the same—
That every prison that men build
  Is built with bricks of shame,
And bound with bars lest Christ should see
  How men their brothers maim.

With bars they blur the gracious moon,
  And blind the goodly sun:
And they do well to hide their Hell,
  For in it things are done
That Son of God nor son of Man

Ever should look upon!

☙❧

The vilest deeds like poison weeds,
    Bloom well in prison-air;
It is only what is good in Man
    That wastes and withers there:
Pale Anguish keeps the heavy gate,
    And the Warder is Despair.

For they starve the little frightened child
    Till it weeps both night and day:
And they scourge the weak, and flog the fool,
    And gibe the old and grey,
And some grow mad, and all grow bad,
    And none a word may say.

Each narrow cell in which we dwell
    Is a foul and dark latrine,
And the fetid breath of living Death
    Chokes up each grated screen,
And all, but Lust, is turned to dust
    In Humanity's machine.

The brackish water that we drink
    Creeps with a loathsome slime,
And the bitter bread they weigh in scales
    Is full of chalk and lime,
And Sleep will not lie down, but walks
    Wild-eyed, and cries to Time.

☙❧

But though lean Hunger and green Thirst
    Like asp with adder fight,
We have little care of prison fare,
    For what chills and kills outright
Is that every stone one lifts by day
    Becomes one's heart by night.

With midnight always in one's heart,
    And twilight in one's cell,

We turn the crank, or tear the rope,
  Each in his separate Hell,
And the silence is more awful far
  Than the sound of a brazen bell.

And never a human voice comes near
  To speak a gentle word:
And the eye that watches through the door
  Is pitiless and hard:
And by all forgot, we rot and rot,
  With soul and body marred.

And thus we rust Life's iron chain
  Degraded and alone:
And some men curse, and some men weep,
  And some men make no moan:
But God's eternal Laws are kind
  And break the heart of stone.

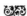

And every human heart that breaks,
  In prison-cell or yard,
Is as that broken box that gave
  Its treasure to the Lord,
And filled the unclean leper's house
  With the scent of costliest nard.

Ah! happy they whose hearts can break
  And peace of pardon win!
How else may man make straight his plan
  And cleanse his soul from Sin?
How else but through a broken heart
  May Lord Christ enter in?

And he of the swollen purple throat,
  And the stark and staring eyes,
Waits for the holy hands that took
  The Thief to Paradise;
And a broken and a contrite heart
  The Lord will not despise.

The man in red who reads the Law
  Gave him three weeks of life,
Three little weeks in which to heal
  His soul of his soul's strife,
And cleanse from every blot of blood
  The hand that held the knife.

And with tears of blood he cleansed the hand,
  The hand that held the steel:
For only blood can wipe out blood,
  And only tears can heal:
And the crimson stain that was of Cain
  Became Christ's snow-white seal.

VI

In Reading gaol by Reading town
    There is a pit of shame,
And in it lies a wretched man
    Eaten by teeth of flame,
In a burning winding-sheet he lies,
    And his grave has got no name.

And there, till Christ call forth the dead,
    In silence let him lie:
No need to waste the foolish tear,
    Or heave the windy sigh:
The man had killed the thing he loved,
    And so he had to die.

And all men kill the thing they love,
    By all let this be heard,
Some do it with a bitter look,
    Some with a flattering word,
The coward does it with a kiss,
    The brave man with a sword!

RAVENNA

I

A year ago I breathed the Italian air,—
And yet, methinks this northern Spring is fair,—
These fields made golden with the flower of March,
The throstle singing on the feathered larch,
The cawing rooks, the wood-doves fluttering by,
The little clouds that race across the sky;
And fair the violet's gentle drooping head,
The primrose, pale for love uncomforted,
The rose that burgeons on the climbing briar,
The crocus-bed, (that seems a moon of fire
Round-girdled with a purple marriage-ring);
And all the flowers of our English Spring,
Fond snowdrops, and the bright-starred daffodil.
Up starts the lark beside the murmuring mill,
And breaks the gossamer-threads of early dew;
And down the river, like a flame of blue,
Keen as an arrow flies the water-king,
While the brown linnets in the greenwood sing.
A year ago!—it seems a little time
Since last I saw that lordly southern clime,
Where flower and fruit to purple radiance blow,
And like bright lamps the fabled apples glow.
Full Spring it was—and by rich flowering vines,
Dark olive-groves and noble forest-pines,
I rode at will; the moist glad air was sweet,
The white road rang beneath my horse's feet,

And musing on Ravenna's ancient name,
I watched the day till, marked with wounds of flame,
The turquoise sky to burnished gold was turned.

O how my heart with boyish passion burned,
When far away across the sedge and mere
I saw that Holy City rising clear,
Crowned with her crown of towers!—On and on
I galloped, racing with the setting sun,
And ere the crimson after-glow was passed,
I stood within Ravenna's walls at last!

I I

How strangely still! no sound of life or joy
Startles the air; no laughing shepherd-boy
Pipes on his reed, nor ever through the day
Comes the glad sound of children at their play:
O sad, and sweet, and silent! surely here
A man might dwell apart from troublous fear,
Watching the tide of seasons as they flow
From amorous Spring to Winter's rain and snow,
And have no thought of sorrow;—here, indeed,
Are Lethe's waters, and that fatal weed
Which makes a man forget his fatherland.

Ay! amid lotus-meadows dost thou stand,
Like Proserpine, with poppy-laden head,
Guarding the holy ashes of the dead.
For though thy brood of warrior sons hath ceased,
Thy noble dead are with thee!—they at least
Are faithful to thine honour:—guard them well,
O childless city! for a mighty spell,
To wake men's hearts to dreams of things sublime,
Are the lone tombs where rest the Great of Time.

III

Yon lonely pillar, rising on the plain,
Marks where the bravest knight of France was slain,—
The Prince of chivalry, the Lord of war,
Gaston de Foix: for some untimely star
Led him against thy city, and he fell,
As falls some forest-lion fighting well.
Taken from life while life and love were new,
He lies beneath God's seamless veil of blue;
Tall lance-like reeds wave sadly o'er his head,
And oleanders bloom to deeper red,
Where his bright youth flowed crimson on the ground.

Look farther north unto that broken mound,—
There, prisoned now within a lordly tomb
Raised by a daughter's hand, in lonely gloom,
Huge-limbed Theodoric, the Gothic king,
Sleeps after all his weary conquering.
Time hath not spared his ruin,—wind and rain
Have broken down his stronghold; and again
We see that Death is mighty lord of all,
And king and clown to ashen dust must fall

Mighty indeed *their* glory! yet to me
Barbaric king, or knight of chivalry,
Or the great queen herself, were poor and vain,
Beside the grave where Dante rests from pain.

His gilded shrine lies open to the air;
And cunning sculptor's hands have carven there
The calm white brow, as calm as earliest morn,
The eyes that flashed with passionate love and scorn,
The lips that sang of Heaven and of Hell,
The almond-face which Giotto drew so well,
The weary face of Dante;—to this day,
Here in his place of resting, far away
From Arno's yellow waters, rushing down
Through the wide bridges of that fairy town,
Where the tall tower of Giotto seems to rise
A marble lily under sapphire skies!

Alas! my Dante! thou hast known the pain
Of meaner lives,—the exile's galling chain,
How steep the stairs within kings' houses are,
And all the petty miseries which mar
Man's nobler nature with the sense of wrong.
Yet this dull world is grateful for thy song;
Our nations do thee homage,—even she,
That cruel queen of vine-clad Tuscany,
Who bound with crown of thorns thy living brow,
Hath decked thine empty tomb with laurels now,
And begs in vain the ashes of her son.

O mightiest exile! all thy grief is done:
Thy soul walks now beside thy Beatrice;
Ravenna guards thine ashes: sleep in peace.

I V

How lone this palace is; how grey the walls!
No minstrel now wakes echoes in these halls.
The broken chain lies rusting on the door,
And noisome weeds have split the marble floor:
Here lurks the snake, and here the lizards run
By the stone lions blinking in the sun.
Byron dwelt here in love and revelry
For two long years—a second Anthony,
Who of the world another Actium made!
Yet suffered not his royal soul to fade,
Or lyre to break, or lance to grow less keen,
'Neath any wiles of an Egyptian queen.
For from the East there came a mighty cry,
And Greece stood up to fight for Liberty,
And called him from Ravenna: never knight
Rode forth more nobly to wild scenes of fight!
None fell more bravely on ensanguined field,
Borne like a Spartan back upon his shield!
O Hellas! Hellas! in thine hour of pride,
Thy day of might, remember him who died
To wrest from off thy limbs the trammelling chain:
O Salamis! O lone Platæan plain!
O tossing waves of wild Euboean sea!
O wind-swept heights of lone Thermopylæ!
He loved you well—ay, not alone in word,
Who freely gave to thee his lyre and sword,

34

Like Æschylos at well-fought Marathon:

And England, too, shall glory in her son,
Her warrior-poet, first in song and fight.
No longer now shall Slander's venomed spite
Crawl like a snake across his perfect name,
Or mar the lordly scutcheon of his fame.

For as the olive-garland of the race,
Which lights with joy each eager runner's face,
As the red cross which saveth men in war,
As a flame-bearded beacon seen from far
By mariners upon a storm-tossed sea,—
Such was his love for Greece and Liberty!

Byron, thy crowns are ever fresh and green:
Red leaves of rose from Sapphic Mitylene
Shall bind thy brows; the myrtle blooms for thee,
In hidden glades by lonely Castaly;
The laurels wait thy coming: all are thine,
And round thy head one perfect wreath will twine.

V

The pine-tops rocked before the evening breeze
With the hoarse murmur of the wintry seas,
And the tall stems were streaked with amber bright;—
I wandered through the wood in wild delight,
Some startled bird, with fluttering wings and fleet,
Made snow of all the blossoms; at my feet,
Like silver crowns, the pale narcissi lay,
And small birds sang on every twining spray.
O waving trees, O forest liberty!
Within your haunts at least a man is free,
And half forgets the weary world of strife:
The blood flows hotter, and a sense of life
Wakes i' the quickening veins, while once again
The woods are filled with gods we fancied slain.
Long time I watched, and surely hoped to see
Some goat-foot Pan make merry minstrelsy
Amid the reeds! some startled Dryad-maid
In girlish flight! or lurking in the glade,
The soft brown limbs, the wanton treacherous face
Of woodland god! Queen Dian in the chase,
White-limbed and terrible, with look of pride,
And leash of boar-hounds leaping at her side!
Or Hylas mirrored in the perfect stream.

O idle heart! O fond Hellenic dream!
Ere long, with melancholy rise and swell,

The evening chimes, the convent's vesper bell,
Struck on mine ears amid the amorous flowers.
Alas! alas! these sweet and honied hours
Had whelmed my heart like some encroaching sea,
And drowned all thoughts of black Gethsemane.

V I

O lone Ravenna! many a tale is told
Of thy great glories in the days of old:
Two thousand years have passed since thou didst see
Cæsar ride forth to royal victory.
Mighty thy name when Rome's lean eagles flew
From Britain's isles to far Euphrates blue;
And of the peoples thou wast noble queen,
Till in thy streets the Goth and Hun were seen.
Discrowned by man, deserted by the sea,
Thou sleepest, rocked in lonely misery!
No longer now upon thy swelling tide,
Pine-forest-like, thy myriad galleys ride!
For where the brass-beaked ships were wont to float,
The weary shepherd pipes his mournful note;
And the white sheep are free to come and go
Where Adria's purple waters used to flow.

O fair! O sad! O Queen uncomforted!
In ruined loveliness thou liest dead,
Alone of all thy sisters; for at last
Italia's royal warrior hath passed
Rome's lordliest entrance, and hath worn his crown
In the high temples of the Eternal Town!
The Palatine hath welcomed back her king,
And with his name the seven mountains ring!

And Naples hath outlived her dream of pain,
And mocks her tyrant! Venice lives again,
New risen from the waters! and the cry
Of Light and Truth, of Love and Liberty,
Is heard in lordly Genoa, and where
The marble spires of Milan wound the air,
Rings from the Alps to the Sicilian shore,
And Dante's dream is now a dream no more.

But thou, Ravenna, better loved than all,
Thy ruined palaces are but a pall
That hides thy fallen greatness! and thy name
Burns like a grey and flickering candle-flame
Beneath the noonday splendour of the sun
Of new Italia! for the night is done,
The night of dark oppression, and the day
Hath dawned in passionate splendour: far away
The Austrian hounds are hunted from the land,
Beyond those ice-crowned citadels which stand
Girdling the plain of royal Lombardy,
From the far West unto the Eastern sea.

I know, indeed, that sons of thine have died
In Lissa's waters, by the mountain-side
Of Aspromonte, on Novara's plain,—
Nor have thy children died for thee in vain:
And yet, methinks, thou hast not drunk this wine
From grapes new-crushed of Liberty divine,
Thou hast not followed that immortal Star
Which leads the people forth to deeds of war.
Weary of life, thou liest in silent sleep,
As one who marks the lengthening shadows creep,
Careless of all the hurrying hours that run,
Mourning some day of glory, for the sun
Of Freedom hath not shewn to thee his face,
And thou hast caught no flambeau in the race.

Yet wake not from thy slumbers,—rest thee well,
Amidst thy fields of amber asphodel,
Thy lily-sprinkled meadows,—rest thee there,
To mock all human greatness: who would dare
To vent the paltry sorrows of his life
Before thy ruins, or to praise the strife

Of kings' ambition, and the barren pride
Of warring nations! wert not thou the Bride
Of the wild Lord of Adria's stormy sea!
The Queen of double Empires! and to thee
Were not the nations given as thy prey!
And now—thy gates lie open night and day,
The grass grows green on every tower and hall,
The ghastly fig hath cleft thy bastioned wall;
And where thy mailèd warriors stood at rest
The midnight owl hath made her secret nest.
O fallen! fallen! from thy high estate,
O city trammelled in the toils of Fate,
Doth nought remain of all thy glorious days,
But a dull shield, a crown of withered bays!

Yet who beneath this night of wars and fears,
From tranquil tower can watch the coming years;
Who can foretell what joys the day shall bring,
Or why before the dawn the linnets sing?
Thou, even thou, mayst wake, as wakes the rose
To crimson splendour from its grave of snows;
As the rich corn-fields rise to red and gold
From these brown lands, now stiff with Winter's cold;
As from the storm-rack comes a perfect star!

O much-loved city! I have wandered far
From the wave-circled islands of my home;
Have seen the gloomy mystery of the Dome
Rise slowly from the drear Campagna's way,
Clothed in the royal purple of the day:
I from the city of the violet crown
Have watched the sun by Corinth's hill go down,
And marked the 'myriad laughter' of the sea
From starlit hills of flower-starred Arcady;
Yet back to thee returns my perfect love,
As to its forest-nest the evening dove.

O poet's city! one who scarce has seen
Some twenty summers cast their doublets green
For Autumn's livery, would seek in vain
To wake his lyre to sing a louder strain,
Or tell thy days of glory;—poor indeed
Is the low murmur of the shepherd's reed,

Where the loud clarion's blast should shake the sky,
And flame across the heavens! and to try
Such lofty themes were folly: yet I know
That never felt my heart a nobler glow
Than when I woke the silence of thy street
With clamorous trampling of my horse's feet,
And saw the city which now I try to sing,
After long days of weary travelling.

VII.

Adieu, Ravenna! but a year ago,
I stood and watched the crimson sunset glow
From the lone chapel on thy marshy plain:
The sky was as a shield that caught the stain
Of blood and battle from the dying sun,
And in the west the circling clouds had spun
A royal robe, which some great God might wear,
While into ocean-seas of purple air
Sank the gold galley of the Lord of Light.

Yet here the gentle stillness of the night
Brings back the swelling tide of memory,
And wakes again my passionate love for thee:
Now is the Spring of Love, yet soon will come
On meadow and tree the Summer's lordly bloom;
And soon the grass with brighter flowers will blow,
And send up lilies for some boy to mow.
Then before long the Summer's conqueror,
Rich Autumn-time, the season's usurer,
Will lend his hoarded gold to all the trees,
And see it scattered by the spendthrift breeze;
And after that the Winter cold and drear.
So runs the perfect cycle of the year.
And so from youth to manhood do we go,
And fall to weary days and locks of snow.
Love only knows no winter; never dies:

Nor cares for frowning storms or leaden skies
And mine for thee shall never pass away,
Though my weak lips may falter in my lay.

Adieu! Adieu! yon silent evening star,
The night's ambassador, doth gleam afar,
And bid the shepherd bring his flocks to fold.
Perchance before our inland seas of gold
Are garnered by the reapers into sheaves,
Perchance before I see the Autumn leaves,
I may behold thy city; and lay down
Low at thy feet the poet's laurel crown.

Adieu! Adieu! yon silver lamp, the moon,
Which turns our midnight into perfect noon,
Doth surely light thy towers, guarding well
Where Dante sleeps, where Byron loved to dwell.

ROSA MYSTICA

REQUIESCAT

Tread lightly, she is near
  Under the snow,
Speak gently, she can hear
  The daisies grow.

All her bright golden hair
  Tarnished with rust,
She that was young and fair
  Fallen to dust.

Lily-like, white as snow,
  She hardly knew
She was a woman, so
  Sweetly she grew.

Coffin-board, heavy stone,
  Lie on her breast,
I vex my heart alone,
  She is at rest.

Peace, Peace, she cannot hear
  Lyre or sonnet,
All my life's buried here,
  Heap earth upon it.

AVIGNON.

SONNET ON APPROACHING ITALY

I reached the Alps: the soul within me burned,
   Italia, my Italia, at thy name:
   And when from out the mountain's heart I came
And saw the land for which my life had yearned,
I laughed as one who some great prize had earned:
   And musing on the marvel of thy fame
   I watched the day, till marked with wounds of flame
The turquoise sky to burnished gold was turned.
The pine-trees waved as waves a woman's hair,
   And in the orchards every twining spray
   Was breaking into flakes of blossoming foam:
But when I knew that far away at Rome
   In evil bonds a second Peter lay,
   I wept to see the land so very fair.

TURIN.

SAN MINIATO

See I have climbed the mountain side
  Up to this holy house of God,
  Where once that Angel-Painter trod
Who saw the heavens opened wide,

And throned upon the crescent moon
  The Virginal white Queen of Grace,—
  Mary! could I but see thy face
Death could not come at all too soon.

O crowned by God with thorns and pain!
  Mother of Christ! O mystic wife!
  My heart is weary of this life
And over-sad to sing again.

O crowned by God with love and flame!
  O crowned by Christ the Holy One!
  O listen ere the searching sun
Show to the world my sin and shame.

AVE MARIA GRATIA PLENA

Was this His coming! I had hoped to see
  A scene of wondrous glory, as was told
  Of some great God who in a rain of gold
Broke open bars and fell on Danae:
Or a dread vision as when Semele
  Sickening for love and unappeased desire
  Prayed to see God's clear body, and the fire
Caught her brown limbs and slew her utterly:
With such glad dreams I sought this holy place,
  And now with wondering eyes and heart I stand
  Before this supreme mystery of Love:
Some kneeling girl with passionless pale face,
  An angel with a lily in his hand,
  And over both the white wings of a Dove.

FLORENCE.

ITALIA

Italia! thou art fallen, though with sheen
   Of battle-spears thy clamorous armies stride
   From the north Alps to the Sicilian tide!
Ay! fallen, though the nations hail thee Queen
Because rich gold in every town is seen,
   And on thy sapphire-lake in tossing pride
   Of wind-filled vans thy myriad galleys ride
Beneath one flag of red and white and green.
O Fair and Strong! O Strong and Fair in vain!
   Look southward where Rome's desecrated town
   Lies mourning for her God-anointed King!
Look heaven-ward! shall God allow this thing?
   Nay! but some flame-girt Raphael shall come down,
   And smite the Spoiler with the sword of pain.

VENICE.

SONNET

WRITTEN IN HOLY WEEK AT GENOA

I wandered through Scoglietto's far retreat,
　　The oranges on each o'erhanging spray
　　Burned as bright lamps of gold to shame the day;
Some startled bird with fluttering wings and fleet
Made snow of all the blossoms; at my feet
　　Like silver moons the pale narcissi lay:
　　And the curved waves that streaked the great green bay
Laughed i' the sun, and life seemed very sweet.
Outside the young boy-priest passed singing clear,
　　'Jesus the son of Mary has been slain,
　　O come and fill His sepulchre with flowers.'
Ah, God!　Ah, God! those dear Hellenic hours
　　Had drowned all memory of Thy bitter pain,
　　The Cross, the Crown, the Soldiers and the Spear.

ROME UNVISITED

The corn has turned from grey to red,
  Since first my spirit wandered forth
  From the drear cities of the north,
And to Italia's mountains fled.

And here I set my face towards home,
  For all my pilgrimage is done,
  Although, methinks, yon blood-red sun
Marshals the way to Holy Rome.

O Blessed Lady, who dost hold
  Upon the seven hills thy reign!
  O Mother without blot or stain,
Crowned with bright crowns of triple gold!

O Roma, Roma, at thy feet
  I lay this barren gift of song!
  For, ah! the way is steep and long
That leads unto thy sacred street.

II.

And yet what joy it were for me
  To turn my feet unto the south,

And journeying towards the Tiber mouth
To kneel again at Fiesole!

And wandering through the tangled pines
　That break the gold of Arno's stream,
　To see the purple mist and gleam
Of morning on the Apennines

By many a vineyard-hidden home,
　Orchard and olive-garden grey,
　Till from the drear Campagna's way
The seven hills bear up the dome!

III.

A pilgrim from the northern seas—
　What joy for me to seek alone
　The wondrous temple and the throne
Of him who holds the awful keys!

When, bright with purple and with gold
　Come priest and holy cardinal,
　And borne above the heads of all
The gentle Shepherd of the Fold.

O joy to see before I die
　The only God-anointed king,
　And hear the silver trumpets ring
A triumph as he passes by!

Or at the brazen-pillared shrine
　Holds high the mystic sacrifice,
　And shows his God to human eyes
Beneath the veil of bread and wine.

IV.

For lo, what changes time can bring!
　The cycles of revolving years
　May free my heart from all its fears,
And teach my lips a song to sing.

Before yon field of trembling gold

Is garnered into dusty sheaves,
  Or ere the autumn's scarlet leaves
Flutter as birds adown the wold,

I may have run the glorious race,
  And caught the torch while yet aflame,
  And called upon the holy name
Of Him who now doth hide His face.

ARONA.

URBS SACRA ÆTERNA

Rome! what a scroll of History thine has been;
  In the first days thy sword republican
  Ruled the whole world for many an age's span:
Then of the peoples wert thou royal Queen,
Till in thy streets the bearded Goth was seen;
  And now upon thy walls the breezes fan
  (Ah, city crowned by God, discrowned by man!)
The hated flag of red and white and green.
When was thy glory! when in search for power
  Thine eagles flew to greet the double sun,
  And the wild nations shuddered at thy rod?
Nay, but thy glory tarried for this hour,
  When pilgrims kneel before the Holy One,
  The prisoned shepherd of the Church of God.

MONTRE MARIO.

SONNET

ON HEARING THE DIES IRÆ SUNG IN THE SISTINE CHAPEL

Nay, Lord, not thus! white lilies in the spring,
Sad olive-groves, or silver-breasted dove,
  Teach me more clearly of Thy life and love
Than terrors of red flame and thundering.
The hillside vines dear memories of Thee bring:
  A bird at evening flying to its nest
  Tells me of One who had no place of rest:
I think it is of Thee the sparrows sing.
Come rather on some autumn afternoon,
  When red and brown are burnished on the leaves,
  And the fields echo to the gleaner's song,
Come when the splendid fulness of the moon
  Looks down upon the rows of golden sheaves,
  And reap Thy harvest: we have waited long.

EASTER DAY

The silver trumpets rang across the Dome:
  The people knelt upon the ground with awe:
  And borne upon the necks of men I saw,
Like some great God, the Holy Lord of Rome.
Priest-like, he wore a robe more white than foam,
  And, king-like, swathed himself in royal red,
  Three crowns of gold rose high upon his head:
In splendour and in light the Pope passed home.
My heart stole back across wide wastes of years
  To One who wandered by a lonely sea,
  And sought in vain for any place of rest:
'Foxes have holes, and every bird its nest.
  I, only I, must wander wearily,
  And bruise my feet, and drink wine salt with tears.'

E TENEBRIS

Come down, O Christ, and help me! reach Thy hand,
  For I am drowning in a stormier sea
  Than Simon on Thy lake of Galilee:
The wine of life is spilt upon the sand,
My heart is as some famine-murdered land
  Whence all good things have perished utterly,
  And well I know my soul in Hell must lie
If I this night before God's throne should stand.
'He sleeps perchance, or rideth to the chase,
  Like Baal, when his prophets howled that name
  From morn to noon on Carmel's smitten height.'
Nay, peace, I shall behold, before the night,
  The feet of brass, the robe more white than flame,
  The wounded hands, the weary human face.

VITA NUOVA

I stood by the unvintageable sea
   Till the wet waves drenched face and hair with spray;
   The long red fires of the dying day
Burned in the west; the wind piped drearily;
And to the land the clamorous gulls did flee:
   'Alas!' I cried, 'my life is full of pain,
   And who can garner fruit or golden grain
From these waste fields which travail ceaselessly!'
My nets gaped wide with many a break and flaw,
   Nathless I threw them as my final cast
   Into the sea, and waited for the end.
When lo! a sudden glory! and I saw
   From the black waters of my tortured past
   The argent splendour of white limbs ascend!

MADONNA MIA

A lilly-girl not made for this world's pain,
  With brown, soft hair close braided by her ears,
  And longing eyes half veiled by slumberous tears
Like bluest water seen through mists of rain:
Pale cheeks whereon no love hath left its stain,
  Red underlip drawn in for fear of love,
  And white throat, whiter than the silvered dove,
Through whose wan marble creeps one purple vein.
Yet, though my lips shall praise her without cease,
  Even to kiss her feet I am not bold,
  Being o'ershadowed by the wings of awe,
Like Dante, when he stood with Beatrice
  Beneath the flaming Lion's breast, and saw
  The seventh Crystal, and the Stair of Gold.

THE NEW HELEN

Where hast thou been since round the walls of Troy
   The sons of God fought in that great emprise?
     Why dost thou walk our common earth again?
Hast thou forgotten that impassioned boy,
   His purple galley and his Tyrian men
   And treacherous Aphrodite's mocking eyes?
For surely it was thou, who, like a star
   Hung in the silver silence of the night,
   Didst lure the Old World's chivalry and might
Into the clamorous crimson waves of war!

Or didst thou rule the fire-laden moon?
   In amorous Sidon was thy temple built
     Over the light and laughter of the sea
   Where, behind lattice scarlet-wrought and gilt,
     Some brown-limbed girl did weave thee tapestry,
All through the waste and wearied hours of noon;
Till her wan cheek with flame of passion burned,
   And she rose up the sea-washed lips to kiss
Of some glad Cyprian sailor, safe returned
   From Calpé and the cliffs of Herakles!

No! thou art Helen, and none other one!
   It was for thee that young Sarpedôn died,
     And Memnôn's manhood was untimely spent;
   It was for thee gold-crested Hector tried

With Thetis' child that evil race to run,
      In the last year of thy beleaguerment;
Ay! even now the glory of thy fame
   Burns in those fields of trampled asphodel,
   Where the high lords whom Ilion knew so well
Clash ghostly shields, and call upon thy name.

Where hast thou been? in that enchanted land
   Whose slumbering vales forlorn Calypso knew,
      Where never mower rose at break of day
   But all unswathed the trammelling grasses grew,
And the sad shepherd saw the tall corn stand
      Till summer's red had changed to withered grey?
Didst thou lie there by some Lethæan stream
   Deep brooding on thine ancient memory,
   The crash of broken spears, the fiery gleam
From shivered helm, the Grecian battle-cry?

Nay, thou wert hidden in that hollow hill
   With one who is forgotten utterly,
      That discrowned Queen men call the Erycine;
   Hidden away that never mightst thou see
The face of Her, before whose mouldering shrine
      To-day at Rome the silent nations kneel;
Who gat from Love no joyous gladdening,
   But only Love's intolerable pain,
   Only a sword to pierce her heart in twain,
Only the bitterness of child-bearing.

The lotus-leaves which heal the wounds of Death
   Lie in thy hand; O, be thou kind to me,
      While yet I know the summer of my days;
   For hardly can my tremulous lips draw breath
To fill the silver trumpet with thy praise,
      So bowed am I before thy mystery;
So bowed and broken on Love's terrible wheel,
   That I have lost all hope and heart to sing,
   Yet care I not what ruin time may bring
If in thy temple thou wilt let me kneel.

Alas, alas, thou wilt not tarry here,
   But, like that bird, the servant of the sun,
      Who flies before the north wind and the night,

So wilt thou fly our evil land and drear,
Back to the tower of thine old delight,
    And the red lips of young Euphorion;
Nor shall I ever see thy face again,
  But in this poisonous garden-close must stay,
  Crowning my brows with the thorn-crown of pain,
Till all my loveless life shall pass away.

O Helen! Helen! Helen! yet a while,
  Yet for a little while, O, tarry here,
    Till the dawn cometh and the shadows flee!
  For in the gladsome sunlight of thy smile
Of heaven or hell I have no thought or fear,
    Seeing I know no other god but thee:
No other god save him, before whose feet
  In nets of gold the tired planets move,
  The incarnate spirit of spiritual love
Who in thy body holds his joyous seat.

Thou wert not born as common women are!
  But, girt with silver splendour of the foam,
    Didst from the depths of sapphire seas arise!
  And at thy coming some immortal star,
Bearded with flame, blazed in the Eastern skies,
    And waked the shepherds on thine island-home.
Thou shalt not die: no asps of Egypt creep
  Close at thy heels to taint the delicate air;
  No sullen-blooming poppies stain thy hair,
Those scarlet heralds of eternal sleep.

Lily of love, pure and inviolate!
  Tower of ivory! red rose of fire!
    Thou hast come down our darkness to illume:
For we, close-caught in the wide nets of Fate,
  Wearied with waiting for the World's Desire,
    Aimlessly wandered in the House of gloom,
Aimlessly sought some slumberous anodyne
  For wasted lives, for lingering wretchedness,
  Till we beheld thy re-arisen shrine,
    And the white glory of thy loveliness.

THE BURDEN OF ITYS

THE BURDEN OF ITYS

This English Thames is holier far than Rome,
  Those harebells like a sudden flush of sea
Breaking across the woodland, with the foam
  Of meadow-sweet and white anemone
To fleck their blue waves,—God is likelier there
Than hidden in that crystal-hearted star the pale monks bear!

Those violet-gleaming butterflies that take
  Yon creamy lily for their pavilion
Are monsignores, and where the rushes shake
  A lazy pike lies basking in the sun,
His eyes half shut,—he is some mitred old
Bishop in *partibus*! look at those gaudy scales all green and gold.

The wind the restless prisoner of the trees
  Does well for Palæstrina, one would say
The mighty master's hands were on the keys
  Of the Maria organ, which they play
When early on some sapphire Easter morn
In a high litter red as blood or sin the Pope is borne

From his dark House out to the Balcony
  Above the bronze gates and the crowded square,
Whose very fountains seem for ecstasy
  To toss their silver lances in the air,
And stretching out weak hands to East and West

In vain sends peace to peaceless lands, to restless nations rest.

Is not yon lingering orange after-glow
   That stays to vex the moon more fair than all
Rome's lordliest pageants! strange, a year ago
   I knelt before some crimson Cardinal
Who bare the Host across the Esquiline,
And now—those common poppies in the wheat seem twice as fine.

The blue-green beanfields yonder, tremulous
   With the last shower, sweeter perfume bring
Through this cool evening than the odorous
   Flame-jewelled censers the young deacons swing,
When the grey priest unlocks the curtained shrine,
And makes God's body from the common fruit of corn and vine.

Poor Fra Giovanni bawling at the mass
   Were out of tune now, for a small brown bird
Sings overhead, and through the long cool grass
   I see that throbbing throat which once I heard
On starlit hills of flower-starred Arcady,
Once where the white and crescent sand of Salamis meets sea.

Sweet is the swallow twittering on the eaves
   At daybreak, when the mower whets his scythe,
And stock-doves murmur, and the milkmaid leaves
   Her little lonely bed, and carols blithe
To see the heavy-lowing cattle wait
Stretching their huge and dripping mouths across the farmyard gate.

And sweet the hops upon the Kentish leas,
   And sweet the wind that lifts the new-mown hay,
And sweet the fretful swarms of grumbling bees
   That round and round the linden blossoms play;
And sweet the heifer breathing in the stall,
And the green bursting figs that hang upon the red-brick wall,

And sweet to hear the cuckoo mock the spring
   While the last violet loiters by the well,
And sweet to hear the shepherd Daphnis sing
   The song of Linus through a sunny dell
Of warm Arcadia where the corn is gold
And the slight lithe-limbed reapers dance about the wattled fold.

And sweet with young Lycoris to recline
　　In some Illyrian valley far away,
Where canopied on herbs amaracine
　　We too might waste the summer-trancèd day
Matching our reeds in sportive rivalry,
While far beneath us frets the troubled purple of the sea.

But sweeter far if silver-sandalled foot
　　Of some long-hidden God should ever tread
The Nuneham meadows, if with reeded flute
　　Pressed to his lips some Faun might raise his head
By the green water-flags, ah! sweet indeed
To see the heavenly herdsman call his white-fleeced flock to feed.

Then sing to me thou tuneful chorister,
　　Though what thou sing'st be thine own requiem!
Tell me thy tale thou hapless chronicler
　　Of thine own tragedies! do not contemn
These unfamiliar haunts, this English field,
For many a lovely coronal our northern isle can yield

Which Grecian meadows know not, many a rose
　　Which all day long in vales Æolian
A lad might seek in vain for over-grows
　　Our hedges like a wanton courtesan
Unthrifty of its beauty; lilies too
Ilissos never mirrored star our streams, and cockles blue

Dot the green wheat which, though they are the signs
　　For swallows going south, would never spread
Their azure tents between the Attic vines;
　　Even that little weed of ragged red,
Which bids the robin pipe, in Arcady
Would be a trespasser, and many an unsung elegy

Sleeps in the reeds that fringe our winding Thames
　　Which to awake were sweeter ravishment
Than ever Syrinx wept for; diadems
　　Of brown bee-studded orchids which were meant
For Cytheræa's brows are hidden here
Unknown to Cytheræa, and by yonder pasturing steer

There is a tiny yellow daffodil,

The butterfly can see it from afar,
Although one summer evening's dew could fill
    Its little cup twice over ere the star
Had called the lazy shepherd to his fold
And be no prodigal; each leaf is flecked with spotted gold

As if Jove's gorgeous leman Danae
    Hot from his gilded arms had stooped to kiss
The trembling petals, or young Mercury
    Low-flying to the dusky ford of Dis
Had with one feather of his pinions
Just brushed them! the slight stem which bears the burden of its suns

Is hardly thicker than the gossamer,
    Or poor Arachne's silver tapestry,—
Men say it bloomed upon the sepulchre
    Of One I sometime worshipped, but to me
It seems to bring diviner memories
Of faun-loved Heliconian glades and blue nymph-haunted seas,

Of an untrodden vale at Tempe where
    On the clear river's marge Narcissus lies,
The tangle of the forest in his hair,
    The silence of the woodland in his eyes,
Wooing that drifting imagery which is
No sooner kissed than broken; memories of Salmacis

Who is not boy nor girl and yet is both,
    Fed by two fires and unsatisfied
Through their excess, each passion being loth
    For love's own sake to leave the other's side
Yet killing love by staying; memories
Of Oreads peeping through the leaves of silent moonlit trees,

Of lonely Ariadne on the wharf
    At Naxos, when she saw the treacherous crew
Far out at sea, and waved her crimson scarf
    And called false Theseus back again nor knew
That Dionysos on an amber pard
Was close behind her; memories of what Mæonia's bard

With sightless eyes beheld, the wall of Troy,
    Queen Helen lying in the ivory room,

And at her side an amorous red-lipped boy
  Trimming with dainty hand his helmet's plume,
And far away the moil, the shout, the groan,
As Hector shielded off the spear and Ajax hurled the stone;

Of wingèd Perseus with his flawless sword
  Cleaving the snaky tresses of the witch,
And all those tales imperishably stored
  In little Grecian urns, freightage more rich
Than any gaudy galleon of Spain
Bare from the Indies ever! these at least bring back again,

For well I know they are not dead at all,
  The ancient Gods of Grecian poesy:
They are asleep, and when they hear thee call
  Will wake and think 't is very Thessaly,
This Thames the Daulian waters, this cool glade
The yellow-irised mead where once young Itys laughed and played.

If it was thou dear jasmine-cradled bird
  Who from the leafy stillness of thy throne
Sang to the wondrous boy, until he heard
  The horn of Atalanta faintly blown
Across the Cumnor hills, and wandering
Through Bagley wood at evening found the Attic poets' spring,—

Ah! tiny sober-suited advocate
  That pleadest for the moon against the day!
If thou didst make the shepherd seek his mate
  On that sweet questing, when Proserpina
Forgot it was not Sicily and leant
Across the mossy Sandford stile in ravished wonderment,—

Light-winged and bright-eyed miracle of the wood!
  If ever thou didst soothe with melody
One of that little clan, that brotherhood
  Which loved the morning-star of Tuscany
More than the perfect sun of Raphael
And is immortal, sing to me! for I too love thee well.

Sing on! sing on! let the dull world grow young,
  Let elemental things take form again,
And the old shapes of Beauty walk among

The simple garths and open crofts, as when
The son of Leto bare the willow rod,
And the soft sheep and shaggy goats followed the boyish God.

Sing on! sing on! and Bacchus will be here
  Astride upon his gorgeous Indian throne,
And over whimpering tigers shake the spear
  With yellow ivy crowned and gummy cone,
While at his side the wanton Bassarid
Will throw the lion by the mane and catch the mountain kid!

Sing on! and I will wear the leopard skin,
  And steal the moonèd wings of Ashtaroth,
Upon whose icy chariot we could win
  Cithæron in an hour ere the froth
Has over-brimmed the wine-vat or the Faun
Ceased from the treading! ay, before the flickering lamp of dawn

Has scared the hooting owlet to its nest,
  And warned the bat to close its filmy vans,
Some Mænad girl with vine-leaves on her breast
  Will filch their beech-nuts from the sleeping Pans
So softly that the little nested thrush
Will never wake, and then with shrilly laugh and leap will rush

Down the green valley where the fallen dew
  Lies thick beneath the elm and count her store,
Till the brown Satyrs in a jolly crew
  Trample the loosestrife down along the shore,
And where their hornèd master sits in state
Bring strawberries and bloomy plums upon a wicker crate!

Sing on! and soon with passion-wearied face
  Through the cool leaves Apollo's lad will come,
The Tyrian prince his bristled boar will chase
  Adown the chestnut-copses all a-bloom,
And ivory-limbed, grey-eyed, with look of pride,
After yon velvet-coated deer the virgin maid will ride.

Sing on! and I the dying boy will see
  Stain with his purple blood the waxen bell
That overweighs the jacinth, and to me
  The wretched Cyprian her woe will tell,

And I will kiss her mouth and streaming eyes,
And lead her to the myrtle-hidden grove where Adon lies!

Cry out aloud on Itys! memory
   That foster-brother of remorse and pain
Drops poison in mine ear,—O to be free,
   To burn one's old ships! and to launch again
Into the white-plumed battle of the waves
And fight old Proteus for the spoil of coral-flowered caves!

O for Medea with her poppied spell!
   O for the secret of the Colchian shrine!
O for one leaf of that pale asphodel
   Which binds the tired brows of Proserpine,
And sheds such wondrous dews at eve that she
Dreams of the fields of Enna, by the far Sicilian sea,

Where oft the golden-girdled bee she chased
   From lily to lily on the level mead,
Ere yet her sombre Lord had bid her taste
   The deadly fruit of that pomegranate seed,
Ere the black steeds had harried her away
Down to the faint and flowerless land, the sick and sunless day.

O for one midnight and as paramour
   The Venus of the little Melian farm!
O that some antique statue for one hour
   Might wake to passion, and that I could charm
The Dawn at Florence from its dumb despair,
Mix with those mighty limbs and make that giant breast my lair!

Sing on! sing on! I would be drunk with life,
   Drunk with the trampled vintage of my youth,
I would forget the wearying wasted strife,
   The riven veil, the Gorgon eyes of Truth,
The prayerless vigil and the cry for prayer,
The barren gifts, the lifted arms, the dull insensate air!

Sing on! sing on! O feathered Niobe,
   Thou canst make sorrow beautiful, and steal
From joy its sweetest music, not as we
   Who by dead voiceless silence strive to heal
Our too untented wounds, and do but keep

73

Pain barricadoed in our hearts, and murder pillowed sleep.

Sing louder yet, why must I still behold
   The wan white face of that deserted Christ,
Whose bleeding hands my hands did once enfold,
   Whose smitten lips my lips so oft have kissed,
And now in mute and marble misery
Sits in his lone dishonoured House and weeps, perchance for me?

O Memory cast down thy wreathèd shell!
   Break thy hoarse lute O sad Melpomene!
O Sorrow, Sorrow keep thy cloistered cell
   Nor dim with tears this limpid Castaly!
Cease, Philomel, thou dost the forest wrong
To vex its sylvan quiet with such wild impassioned song!

Cease, cease, or if 't is anguish to be dumb
   Take from the pastoral thrush her simpler air,
Whose jocund carelessness doth more become
   This English woodland than thy keen despair,
Ah! cease and let the north wind bear thy lay
Back to the rocky hills of Thrace, the stormy Daulian bay.

A moment more, the startled leaves had stirred,
   Endymion would have passed across the mead
Moonstruck with love, and this still Thames had heard
   Pan plash and paddle groping for some reed
To lure from her blue cave that Naiad maid
Who for such piping listens half in joy and half afraid.

A moment more, the waking dove had cooed,
   The silver daughter of the silver sea
With the fond gyves of clinging hands had wooed
   Her wanton from the chase, and Dryope
Had thrust aside the branches of her oak
To see the lusty gold-haired lad rein in his snorting yoke.

A moment more, the trees had stooped to kiss
   Pale Daphne just awakening from the swoon
Of tremulous laurels, lonely Salmacis
   Had bared his barren beauty to the moon,
And through the vale with sad voluptuous smile
Antinous had wandered, the red lotus of the Nile

Down leaning from his black and clustering hair,
  To shade those slumberous eyelids' caverned bliss,
Or else on yonder grassy slope with bare
  High-tuniced limbs unravished Artemis
Had bade her hounds give tongue, and roused the deer
From his green ambuscade with shrill halloo and pricking spear.

Lie still, lie still, O passionate heart, lie still!
  O Melancholy, fold thy raven wing!
O sobbing Dryad, from thy hollow hill
  Come not with such despondent answering!
No more thou wingèd Marsyas complain,
Apollo loveth not to hear such troubled songs of pain!

It was a dream, the glade is tenantless,
  No soft Ionian laughter moves the air,
The Thames creeps on in sluggish leadenness,
  And from the copse left desolate and bare
Fled is young Bacchus with his revelry,
Yet still from Nuneham wood there comes that thrilling melody

So sad, that one might think a human heart
  Brake in each separate note, a quality
Which music sometimes has, being the Art
  Which is most nigh to tears and memory;
Poor mourning Philomel, what dost thou fear?
Thy sister doth not haunt these fields, Pandion is not here,

Here is no cruel Lord with murderous blade,
  No woven web of bloody heraldries,
But mossy dells for roving comrades made,
  Warm valleys where the tired student lies
With half-shut book, and many a winding walk
Where rustic lovers stray at eve in happy simple talk.

The harmless rabbit gambols with its young
  Across the trampled towing-path, where late
A troop of laughing boys in jostling throng
  Cheered with their noisy cries the racing eight;
The gossamer, with ravelled silver threads,
Works at its little loom, and from the dusky red-eaved sheds

Of the lone Farm a flickering light shines out

Where the swinked shepherd drives his bleating flock
Back to their wattled sheep-cotes, a faint shout
  Comes from some Oxford boat at Sandford lock,
And starts the moor-hen from the sedgy rill,
And the dim lengthening shadows flit like swallows up the hill.

The heron passes homeward to the mere,
  The blue mist creeps among the shivering trees,
Gold world by world the silent stars appear,
  And like a blossom blown before the breeze
A white moon drifts across the shimmering sky,
Mute arbitress of all thy sad, thy rapturous threnody.

She does not heed thee, wherefore should she heed,
  She knows Endymion is not far away;
'Tis I, 'tis I, whose soul is as the reed
  Which has no message of its own to play,
So pipes another's bidding, it is I,
Drifting with every wind on the wide sea of misery.

Ah! the brown bird has ceased: one exquisite trill
  About the sombre woodland seems to cling
Dying in music, else the air is still,
  So still that one might hear the bat's small wing
Wander and wheel above the pines, or tell
Each tiny dew-drop dripping from the bluebell's brimming cell.

And far away across the lengthening wold,
  Across the willowy flats and thickets brown,
Magdalen's tall tower tipped with tremulous gold
  Marks the long High Street of the little town,
And warns me to return; I must not wait,
Hark! 't is the curfew booming from the bell at Christ Church gate.

THE SPHINX

THE SPHINX

In a dim corner of my room for longer than my fancy thinks
A beautiful and silent Sphinx has watched me through the shifting
gloom.

Inviolate and immobile she does not rise she does not stir
For silver moons are naught to her and naught to her the suns that
reel.

Red follows grey across the air, the waves of moonlight ebb and flow
But with the Dawn she does not go and in the night-time she is there.

Dawn follows Dawn and Nights grow old and all the while this
curious cat
Lies couching on the Chinese mat with eyes of satin rimmed with
gold.

Upon the mat she lies and leers and on the tawny throat of her
Flutters the soft and silky fur or ripples to her pointed ears.

Come forth, my lovely seneschal! so somnolent, so statuesque!
Come forth you exquisite grotesque! half woman and half animal!

Come forth my lovely languorous Sphinx! and put your head upon
my knee!
And let me stroke your throat and see your body spotted like the
Lynx!

And let me touch those curving claws of yellow ivory and grasp
The tail that like a monstrous Asp coils round your heavy velvet
paws!

A thousand weary centuries are thine while I have hardly seen
Some twenty summers cast their green for Autumn's gaudy liveries.

But you can read the Hieroglyphs on the great sandstone obelisks,
And you have talked with Basilisks, and you have looked on
Hippogriffs.

O tell me, were you standing by when Isis to Osiris knelt?
And did you watch the Egyptian melt her union for Antony

And drink the jewel-drunken wine and bend her head in mimic awe
To see the huge proconsul draw the salted tunny from the brine?

And did you mark the Cyprian kiss white Adon on his catafalque?
And did you follow Amenalk, the God of Heliopolis?

And did you talk with Thoth, and did you hear the moon-horned Io
weep?
And know the painted kings who sleep beneath the wedge-shaped
Pyramid?

Lift up your large black satin eyes which are like cushions where one
sinks!
Fawn at my feet, fantastic Sphinx! and sing me all your memories!

Sing to me of the Jewish maid who wandered with the Holy Child,
And how you led them through the wild, and how they slept beneath
your shade.

Sing to me of that odorous green eve when crouching by the marge
You heard from Adrian's gilded barge the laughter of Antinous

And lapped the stream and fed your drouth and watched with hot
and hungry stare
The ivory body of that rare young slave with his pomegranate
mouth!

Sing to me of the Labyrinth in which the twi-formed bull was stalled!
Sing to me of the night you crawled across the temple's granite plinth

When through the purple corridors the screaming scarlet Ibis flew
In terror, and a horrid dew dripped from the moaning Mandragores,

And the great torpid crocodile within the tank shed slimy tears,
And tare the jewels from his ears and staggered back into the Nile,

And the priests cursed you with shrill psalms as in your claws you
    seized their snake
And crept away with it to slake your passion by the shuddering
    palms.

Who were your lovers? who were they who wrestled for you in the
    dust?
Which was the vessel of your Lust? What Leman had you,
    every day?

Did giant Lizards come and crouch before you on the reedy banks?
Did Gryphons with great metal flanks leap on you in your trampled
    couch?

Did monstrous hippopotami come sidling toward you in the mist?
Did gilt-scaled dragons writhe and twist with passion as you passed
    them by?

And from the brick-built Lycian tomb what horrible Chimera came
With fearful heads and fearful flame to breed new wonders from
    your womb?

Or had you shameful secret quests and did you harry to your home
Some Nereid coiled in amber foam with curious rock crystal breasts?

Or did you treading through the froth call to the brown Sidonian
For tidings of Leviathan, Leviathan or Behemoth?

Or did you when the sun was set climb up the cactus-covered slope
To meet your swarthy Ethiop whose body was of polished jet?

Or did you while the earthen skiffs dropped down the grey Nilotic
    flats
At twilight and the flickering bats flew round the temple's triple
    glyphs

Steal to the border of the bar and swim across the silent lake

And slink into the vault and make the Pyramid your lúpanar

Till from each black sarcophagus rose up the painted swathèd dead?
Or did you lure unto your bed the ivory-horned Tragelaphos?

Or did you love the god of flies who plagued the Hebrews and was
    splashed
With wine unto the waist? or Pasht, who had green beryls for her
    eyes?

Or that young god, the Tyrian, who was more amorous than the dove
Of Ashtaroth? or did you love the god of the Assyrian

Whose wings, like strange transparent talc, rose high above his hawk-
    faced head,
Painted with silver and with red and ribbed with rods of Oreichalch?

Or did huge Apis from his car leap down and lay before your feet
Big blossoms of the honey-sweet and honey-coloured nenuphar?

How subtle-secret is your smile! Did you love none then? Nay,
    I know
Great Ammon was your bedfellow! He lay with you beside the Nile!

The river-horses in the slime trumpeted when they saw him come
Odorous with Syrian galbanum and smeared with spikenard and
    with thyme.

He came along the river bank like some tall galley argent-sailed,
He strode across the waters, mailed in beauty, and the waters sank.

He strode across the desert sand: he reached the valley where
    you lay:
He waited till the dawn of day: then touched your black breasts with
    his hand.

You kissed his mouth with mouths of flame: you made the hornèd
    god your own:
You stood behind him on his throne: you called him by his secret
    name.

You whispered monstrous oracles into the caverns of his ears:

With blood of goats and blood of steers you taught him monstrous
    miracles.

White Ammon was your bedfellow! Your chamber was the steaming
    Nile!
And with your curved archaic smile you watched his passion come
    and go.

With Syrian oils his brows were bright: and wide-spread as a tent
    at noon
His marble limbs made pale the moon and lent the day a larger light.

His long hair was nine cubits' span and coloured like that yellow gem
Which hidden in their garment's hem the merchants bring from
    Kurdistan.

His face was as the must that lies upon a vat of new-made wine:
The seas could not insapphirine the perfect azure of his eyes.

His thick soft throat was white as milk and threaded with thin veins
    of blue:
And curious pearls like frozen dew were broidered on his flowing
    silk.

On pearl and porphyry pedestalled he was too bright to look upon:
For on his ivory breast there shone the wondrous ocean-emerald,

That mystic moonlit jewel which some diver of the Colchian caves
Had found beneath the blackening waves and carried to the Colchian
    witch.

Before his gilded galiot ran naked vine-wreathed corybants,
And lines of swaying elephants knelt down to draw his chariot,

And lines of swarthy Nubians bare up his litter as he rode
Down the great granite-paven road between the nodding peacock-
    fans.

The merchants brought him steatite from Sidon in their painted ships:
The meanest cup that touched his lips was fashioned from a
    chrysolite.

The merchants brought him cedar chests of rich apparel bound with
    cords:
His train was borne by Memphian lords: young kings were glad to be
    his guests.

Ten hundred shaven priests did bow to Ammon's altar day and
    night,
Ten hundred lamps did wave their light through Ammon's carven
    house—and now

Foul snake and speckled adder with their young ones crawl from
    stone to stone
For ruined is the house and prone the great rose-marble monolith!

Wild ass or trotting jackal comes and couches in the mouldering
    gates:
Wild satyrs call unto their mates across the fallen fluted drums.

And on the summit of the pile the blue-faced ape of Horus sits
And gibbers while the fig-tree splits the pillars of the peristyle

The god is scattered here and there: deep hidden in the windy sand
I saw his giant granite hand still clenched in impotent despair.

And many a wandering caravan of stately negroes silken-shawled,
Crossing the desert, halts appalled before the neck that none can
    span.

And many a bearded Bedouin draws back his yellow-striped
    burnous
To gaze upon the Titan thews of him who was thy paladin.

Go, seek his fragments on the moor and wash them in the evening
    dew,
And from their pieces make anew thy mutilated paramour!

Go, seek them where they lie alone and from their broken
    pieces make
Thy bruisèd bedfellow! And wake mad passions in the senseless
    stone!

Charm his dull ear with Syrian hymns! he loved your body! oh, be
    kind,

Pour spikenard on his hair, and wind soft rolls of linen round his
limbs!

Wind round his head the figured coins! stain with red fruits those
pallid lips!
Weave purple for his shrunken hips! and purple for his barren loins!

Away to Egypt! Have no fear. Only one God has ever died.
Only one God has let His side be wounded by a soldier's spear.

But these, thy lovers, are not dead. Still by the hundred-cubit gate
Dog-faced Anubis sits in state with lotus-lilies for thy head.

Still from his chair of porphyry gaunt Memnon strains his lidless eyes
Across the empty land, and cries each yellow morning unto thee.

And Nilus with his broken horn lies in his black and oozy bed
And till thy coming will not spread his waters on the withering corn.

Your lovers are not dead, I know. They will rise up and hear your
voice
And clash their cymbals and rejoice and run to kiss your mouth!
And so,

Set wings upon your argosies! Set horses to your ebon car!
Back to your Nile! Or if you are grown sick of dead divinities

Follow some roving lion's spoor across the copper-coloured plain,
Reach out and hale him by the mane and bid him be your paramour!

Couch by his side upon the grass and set your white teeth in his
throat
And when you hear his dying note lash your long flanks of polished
brass

And take a tiger for your mate, whose amber sides are flecked with
black,
And ride upon his gilded back in triumph through the Theban gate,

And toy with him in amorous jests, and when he turns, and snarls,
and gnaws,
O smite him with your jasper claws! and bruise him with your agate
breasts!

Why are you tarrying? Get hence! I weary of your sullen ways,
I weary of your steadfast gaze, your somnolent magnificence.

Your horrible and heavy breath makes the light flicker in the lamp,
And on my brow I feel the damp and dreadful dews of night and
    death.

Your eyes are like fantastic moons that shiver in some stagnant lake,
Your tongue is like a scarlet snake that dances to fantastic tunes,

Your pulse makes poisonous melodies, and your black throat is like
    the hole
Left by some torch or burning coal on Saracenic tapestries.

Away! The sulphur-coloured stars are hurrying through the Western
    gate!
Away! Or it may be too late to climb their silent silver cars!

See, the dawn shivers round the grey gilt-dialled towers, and the rain
Streams down each diamonded pane and blurs with tears the
    wannish day.

What snake-tressed fury fresh from Hell, with uncouth gestures and
    unclean,
Stole from the poppy-drowsy queen and led you to a student's cell?

What songless tongueless ghost of sin crept through the curtains of
    the night,
And saw my taper burning bright, and knocked, and bade you
    enter in?

Are there not others more accursed, whiter with leprosies than I?
Are Abana and Pharphar dry that you come here to slake your thirst?

Get hence, you loathsome mystery! Hideous animal, get hence!
You wake in me each bestial sense, you make me what I would
    not be.

You make my creed a barren sham, you wake foul dreams of sensual
    life,
And Atys with his blood-stained knife were better than the thing
    I am.

False Sphinx! False Sphinx! By reedy Styx old Charon, leaning on
    his oar,
Waits for my coin. Go thou before, and leave me to my crucifix,

Whose pallid burden, sick with pain, watches the world with wearied
    eyes,
And weeps for every soul that dies, and weeps for every soul in vain

FLOWERS OF GOLD

IMPRESSIONS

I
LES SILHOUETTES

The sea is flecked with bars of grey,
  The dull dead wind is out of tune,
  And like a withered leaf the moon
Is blown across the stormy bay.

Etched clear upon the pallid sand
  Lies the black boat: a sailor boy
  Clambers aboard in careless joy
With laughing face and gleaming hand.

And overhead the curlews cry,
  Where through the dusky upland grass
  The young brown-throated reapers pass,
Like silhouettes against the sky.

II
LA FUITE DE LA LUNE

To outer senses there is peace,
  A dreamy peace on either hand
  Deep silence in the shadowy land,
Deep silence where the shadows cease.

Save for a cry that echoes shrill
  From some lone bird disconsolate;
  A corncrake calling to its mate;
The answer from the misty hill.

And suddenly the moon withdraws
  Her sickle from the lightening skies,
  And to her sombre cavern flies,
Wrapped in a veil of yellow gauze.

THE GRAVE OF KEATS

Rid of the world's injustice, and his pain,
  He rests at last beneath God's veil of blue:
  Taken from life when life and love were new
The youngest of the martyrs here is lain,
Fair as Sebastian, and as early slain.
  No cypress shades his grave, no funeral yew,
  But gentle violets weeping with the dew
Weave on his bones an ever-blossoming chain.
O proudest heart that broke for misery!
  O sweetest lips since those of Mitylene!
  O poet-painter of our English Land!
Thy name was writ in water—it shall stand:
  And tears like mine will keep thy memory green,
  As Isabella did her Basil-tree.

ROME.

THEOCRITUS

A VILLANELLE

O singer of Persephone!
  In the dim meadows desolate
Dost thou remember Sicily?

Still through the ivy flits the bee
  Where Amaryllis lies in state;
O Singer of Persephone!

Simætha calls on Hecate
  And hears the wild dogs at the gate;
Dost thou remember Sicily?

Still by the light and laughing sea
  Poor Polypheme bemoans his fate;
O Singer of Persephone!

And still in boyish rivalry
  Young Daphnis challenges his mate;
Dost thou remember Sicily?

Slim Lacon keeps a goat for thee,
  For thee the jocund shepherds wait;
O Singer of Persephone!
Dost thou remember Sicily?

IN THE GOLD ROOM

A HARMONY

Her ivory hands on the ivory keys
  Strayed in a fitful fantasy,
Like the silver gleam when the poplar trees
  Rustle their pale-leaves listlessly,
Or the drifting foam of a restless sea
When the waves show their teeth in the flying breeze.

Her gold hair fell on the wall of gold
  Like the delicate gossamer tangles spun
On the burnished disk of the marigold,
  Or the sunflower turning to meet the sun
  When the gloom of the dark blue night is done,
And the spear of the lily is aureoled.

And her sweet red lips on these lips of mine
  Burned like the ruby fire set
In the swinging lamp of a crimson shrine,
  Or the bleeding wounds of the pomegranate,
  Or the heart of the lotus drenched and wet
With the spilt-out blood of the rose-red wine.

BALLADE DE MARGUERITE

(NORMANDE)

I am weary of lying within the chase
When the knights are meeting in market-place.

Nay, go not thou to the red-roofed town
Lest the hoofs of the war-horse tread thee down.

But I would not go where the Squires ride,
I would only walk by my Lady's side.

Alack! and alack! thou art overbold,
A Forester's son may not eat off gold.

Will she love me the less that my Father is seen
Each Martinmas day in a doublet green?

Perchance she is sewing at tapestrie,
Spindle and loom are not meet for thee.

Ah, if she is working the arras bright
I might ravel the threads by the fire-light.

Perchance she is hunting of the deer,
How could you follow o'er hill and mere?

Ah, if she is riding with the court,
I might run beside her and wind the morte.

Perchance she is kneeling in St. Denys,
(On her soul may our Lady have gramercy!)

Ah, if she is praying in lone chapelle,
I might swing the censer and ring the bell.

Come in, my son, for you look sae pale,
The father shall fill thee a stoup of ale.

But who are these knights in bright array?
Is it a pageant the rich folks play?

'T is the King of England from over sea,
Who has come unto visit our fair countrie.

But why does the curfew toll sae low?
And why do the mourners walk a-row?

O 't is Hugh of Amiens my sister's son
Who is lying stark, for his day is done.

Nay, nay, for I see white lilies clear,
It is no strong man who lies on the bier.

O 't is old Dame Jeannette that kept the hall,
I knew she would die at the autumn fall.

Dame Jeannette had not that gold-brown hair,
Old Jeannette was not a maiden fair.

O 't is none of our kith and none of our kin,
(Her soul may our Lady assoil from sin!)

But I hear the boy's voice chaunting sweet,
'Elle est morte, la Marguerite.'

Come in, my son, and lie on the bed,
And let the dead folk bury their dead.

O mother, you know I loved her true:
O mother, hath one grave room for two?

THE DOLE OF THE KING'S DAUGHTER

(BRETON)

Seven stars in the still water,
   And seven in the sky;
Seven sins on the King's daughter,
   Deep in her soul to lie.

Red roses are at her feet,
   (Roses are red in her red-gold hair)
And O where her bosom and girdle meet
   Red roses are hidden there.

Fair is the knight who lieth slain
   Amid the rush and reed,
See the lean fishes that are fain
   Upon dead men to feed.

Sweet is the page that lieth there,
   (Cloth of gold is goodly prey,)
See the black ravens in the air,
   Black, O black as the night are they.

What do they there so stark and dead?
   (There is blood upon her hand)
Why are the lilies flecked with red?
   (There is blood on the river sand.)

There are two that ride from the south and east,

And two from the north and west,
For the black raven a goodly feast,
  For the King's daughter rest.

There is one man who loves her true,
  (Red, O red, is the stain of gore!)
He hath duggen a grave by the darksome yew,
  (One grave will do for four.)

No moon in the still heaven,
  In the black water none,
The sins on her soul are seven,
  The sin upon his is one.

A VISION

Two crownèd Kings, and One that stood alone
　　With no green weight of laurels round his head,
　　But with sad eyes as one uncomforted,
And wearied with man's never-ceasing moan
For sins no bleating victim can atone,
　　And sweet long lips with tears and kisses fed.
　　Girt was he in a garment black and red,
And at his feet I marked a broken stone
　　Which sent up lilies, dove-like, to his knees.
Now at their sight, my heart being lit with flame,
I cried to Beatricé, 'Who are these?'
And she made answer, knowing well each name,
　　'Æschylos first, the second Sophokles,
　　And last (wide stream of tears!) Euripides.'

AMOR INTELLECTUALIS

Oft have we trod the vales of Castaly
  And heard sweet notes of sylvan music blown
  From antique reeds to common folk unknown:
And often launched our bark upon that sea
Which the nine Muses hold in empery,
  And ploughed free furrows through the wave and foam,
  Nor spread reluctant sail for more safe home
Till we had freighted well our argosy.
Of which despoilèd treasures these remain,
  Sordello's passion, and the honeyed line
Of young Endymion, lordly Tamburlaine
  Driving his pampered jades, and more than these,
The seven-fold vision of the Florentine,
  And grave-browed Milton's solemn harmonies.

SANTA DECCA

The Gods are dead: no longer do we bring
  To grey-eyed Pallas crowns of olive-leaves!
  Demeter's child no more hath tithe of sheaves,
And in the noon the careless shepherds sing,
For Pan is dead, and all the wantoning
  By secret glade and devious haunt is o'er:
  Young Hylas seeks the water-springs no more;
Great Pan is dead, and Mary's son is King.

And yet—perchance in this sea-trancèd isle,
  Chewing the bitter fruit of memory,
  Some God lies hidden in the asphodel.
Ah Love! if such there be, then it were well
  For us to fly his anger: nay, but see,
  The leaves are stirring: let us watch awhile.

CORFU.

IMPRESSION DE VOYAGE

The sea was sapphire coloured, and the sky
   Burned like a heated opal through the air;
   We hoisted sail; the wind was blowing fair
For the blue lands that to the eastward lie.
From the steep prow I marked with quickening eye
   Zakynthos, every olive grove and creek,
   Ithaca's cliff, Lycaon's snowy peak,
And all the flower-strewn hills of Arcady.
   The flapping of the sail against the mast,
   The ripple of the water on the side,
The ripple of girls' laughter at the stern,
The only sounds:—when 'gan the West to burn,
   And a red sun upon the seas to ride,
   I stood upon the soil of Greece at last!

KATAKOLO.

THE GRAVE OF SHELLEY

Like burnt-out torches by a sick man's bed
   Gaunt cypress-trees stand round the sun-bleached stone;
   Here doth the little night-owl make her throne,
And the slight lizard show his jewelled head.
And, where the chaliced poppies flame to red,
   In the still chamber of yon pyramid
   Surely some Old-World Sphinx lurks darkly hid,
Grim warder of this pleasaunce of the dead.

Ah! sweet indeed to rest within the womb
   Of Earth, great mother of eternal sleep,
But sweeter far for thee a restless tomb
   In the blue cavern of an echoing deep,
Or where the tall ships founder in the gloom
   Against the rocks of some wave-shattered steep.

ROME.

BY THE ARNO

The oleander on the wall
  Grows crimson in the dawning light,
  Though the grey shadows of the night
Lie yet on Florence like a pall.

The dew is bright upon the hill,
  And bright the blossoms overhead,
  But ah! the grasshoppers have fled,
The little Attic song is still.

Only the leaves are gently stirred
  By the soft breathing of the gale,
  And in the almond-scented vale
The lonely nightingale is heard.

The day will make thee silent soon,
  O nightingale sing on for love!
  While yet upon the shadowy grove
Splinter the arrows of the moon.

Before across the silent lawn
  In sea-green vest the morning steals,
  And to love's frightened eyes reveals
The long white fingers of the dawn

Fast climbing up the eastern sky
   To grasp and slay the shuddering night,
   All careless of my heart's delight,
Or if the nightingale should die.

Made in the USA
Middletown, DE
25 November 2020